Make it with

Paper

BOOK  HOUSE

©Copyright for the English edition for the UK and British Commonwealth by Book House

Original title: ¡Vamos a Crear! Papel
©Parramon Ediciones, S.A., 2000

All rights reserved. No other part of this book may be reproduced, stored in a retrieval system or transmitted in any form or by any means, electronic, mechanical, photocopying, recording or otherwise, without the written permission of the copyright owner.

Published in Great Britain in 2003 by Book House, an imprint of
The Salariya Book Company Ltd
25 Marlborough Place, Brighton BN1 1UB

Please visit the Salariya Book Company at:
www.salariya.com
www.book-house.co.uk

ISBN 1 904194 94 X

A catalogue record for this book is available from the British Library.

Printed and bound in Spain.

Contents

Introduction

Introduction

Most paper is made from a mixture of plant fibres and is sold in thin sheets, but different kinds of paper are made for different purposes. Some kinds of paper are made especially for drawing. Paper called stationery is made for writing. Waxed paper and cellophane are made for wrapping food. Tissue paper is made to be very soft, so it is the best kind of paper for napkins, paper towels and toilet paper.

The kinds of paper you will need for the projects in this book can all be used for the same purpose – to create crafts. This book contains twelve simple crafts made with paper, including a handy booklet with a collage on the cover, a colourful clown doll, a curvy cat and some fabulous flowers. All of the projects are meant to be a starting point for inventing your own paper creations.

Because paper is a material that is used so often and for so many purposes, finding it at home or in school should be very easy. To work with paper, you need only scissors, a glue stick, tape and a few other simple, easy-to-find supplies.

The kinds of paper you will use range from the simple white sheets to aluminium foil and include thin tissue paper, thick construction paper, stretchy crepe paper and crinkly cellophane. Some projects call for cardboard in particular colours. If you have white cardboard, however, you can colour it yourself with crayons, coloured pencils, or paints.

Watch for special instructions at the end of each project to try other great ideas. Sometimes, making just one small change creates a very different result. Start creating craft surprises with paper of all kinds and sizes!

**REMEMBER!
Whenever you see this symbol, or when you are using scissors, ask an adult to help you.**

Collage-covered
Booklet

Collage-covered
Booklet

Collage-covered
Booklet

Collage-covered Booklet

Making an apple collage is as easy as pie and adds an artistic flair to this useful little concertina-stlye booklet.

Toolbox

You will need:

- A4 (210 mm x 297 mm) sheets of paper in many different colours
- coloured felt-tip
- glue stick
- scissors
- ruler

1 Cut a piece of paper so it measures 10 x 10 cm and draw an apple on it with a coloured felt-tip.

2 Cut many small scraps out of different coloured sheets of paper.

3 Glue blue paper scraps around the outside of the apple and red scraps inside the apple. Make a leaf out of green paper and glue it onto the apple.

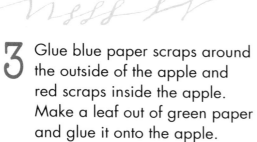

4 Fold four sheets of paper in half, lengthwise. Each sheet of paper should be a different colour. Cut along the folds to make strips.

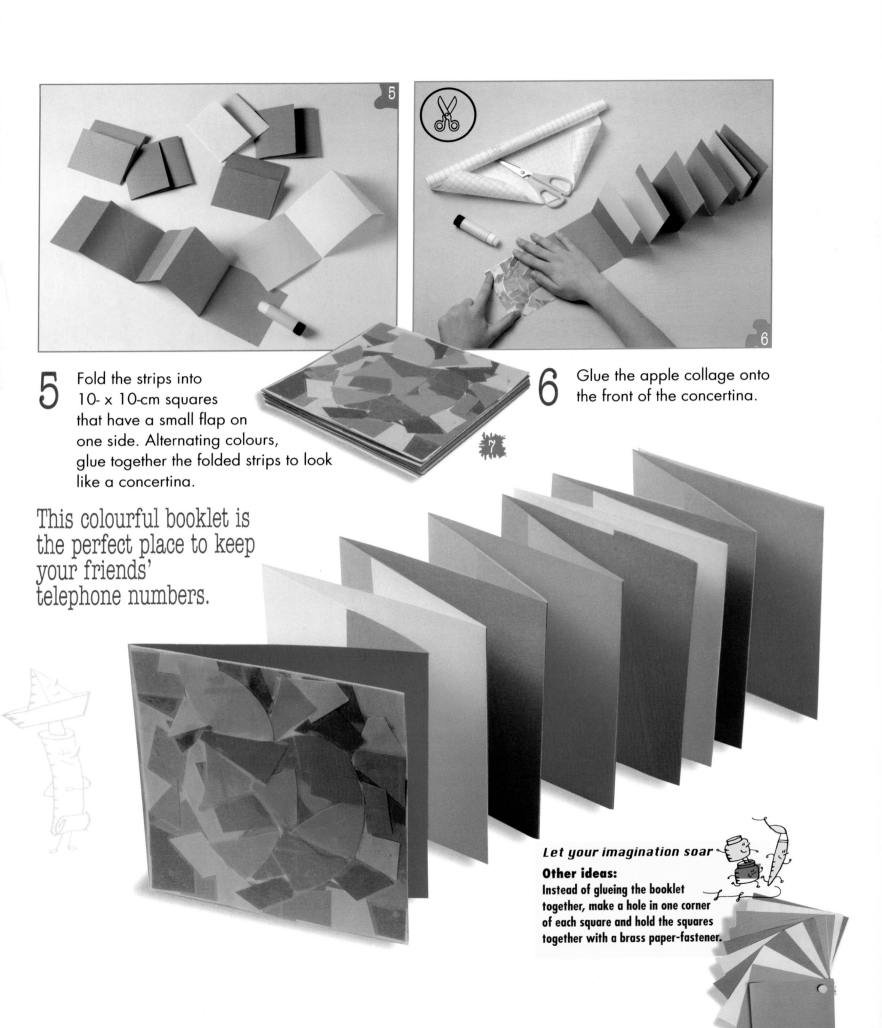

5 Fold the strips into 10- x 10-cm squares that have a small flap on one side. Alternating colours, glue together the folded strips to look like a concertina.

This colourful booklet is the perfect place to keep your friends' telephone numbers.

6 Glue the apple collage onto the front of the concertina.

Let your imagination soar

Other ideas:
Instead of glueing the booklet together, make a hole in one corner of each square and hold the squares together with a brass paper-fastener.

Carnival Hat

Tissue paper polka dots and a paper garland fringe can turn a plain party hat into a flashy carnival decoration.

1 Use a pair of compasses and a ruler to draw a large half circle on a piece of yellow cardboard. Cut out the half circle and roll it into the shape of a cone. Glue it together so it looks like an ice-cream cone.

2 Cut out circles of pink, green and orange tissue paper. You can make a lot of circles at one time by folding a piece of tissue paper many times, then cutting one circle through all the folded layers.

Toolbox

You will need:

- pair of compasses
- pink, green and orange tissue paper
- yellow cardboard
- yellow paper garland
- latex glue
- paintbrush
- ruler
- glue stick
- scissors

3 Mix latex glue with a little water. Brush glue onto the tissue paper circles, one at a time, and stick each circle onto the yellow cone.

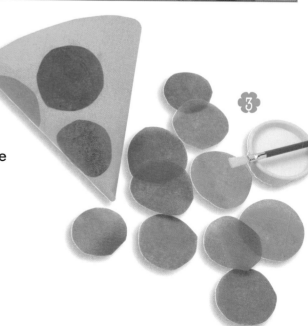

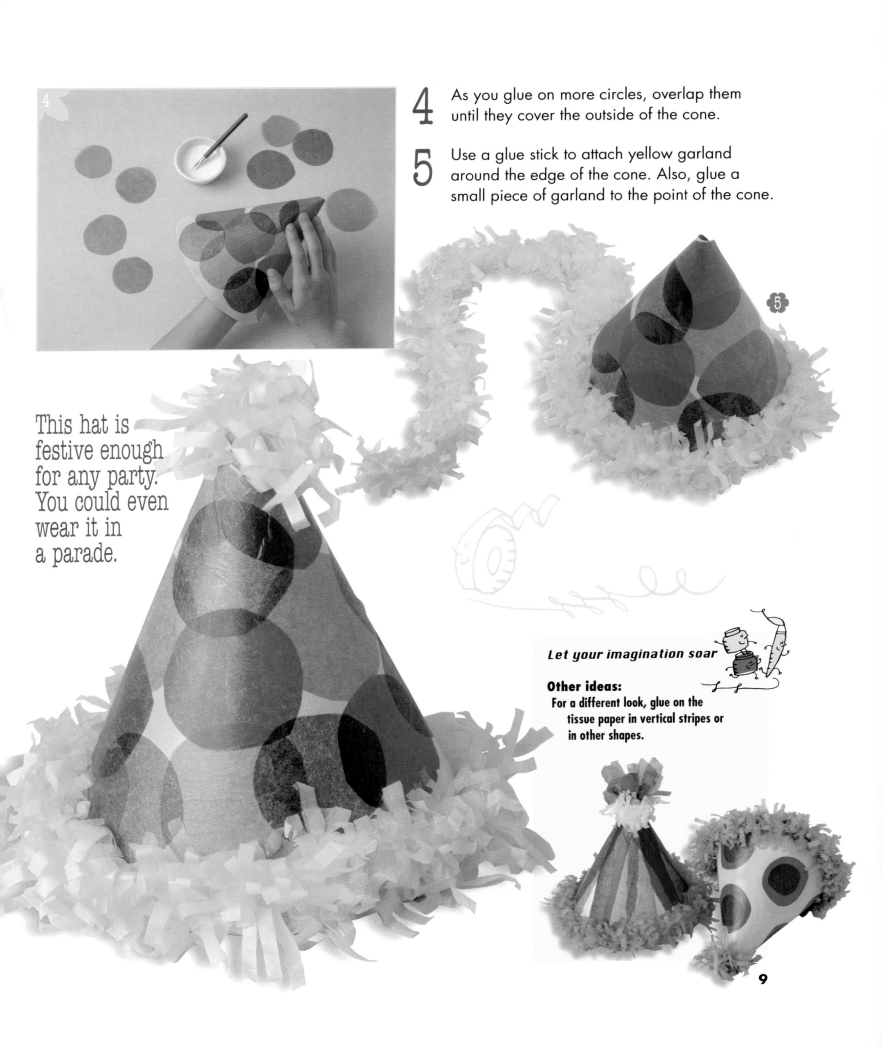

4 As you glue on more circles, overlap them until they cover the outside of the cone.

5 Use a glue stick to attach yellow garland around the edge of the cone. Also, glue a small piece of garland to the point of the cone.

This hat is festive enough for any party. You could even wear it in a parade.

Let your imagination soar

Other ideas:
For a different look, glue on the tissue paper in vertical stripes or in other shapes.

Colourful Clown

This cute clown is dressed for the circus, but with a piece of blue string attached to his head, he's happy to hang around with you instead.

Toolbox

You will need:
- thin, pointed, wooden stick
- white, red, blue and flesh-coloured paints
- multicoloured paper garland
- table-tennis ball
- orange paper garland
- blue string
- scissors
- red crepe paper
- paintbrush
- sewing needle
- glue stick

1 To make the head, push the point of a thin wooden stick into a table-tennis ball. Brush flesh-coloured paint over the ball and let it dry. Paint eyes, a nose and a mouth on the ball with white, red and blue paints.

2 Cut two pieces of multi-coloured garland. Make one of the pieces longer than the other. Tie the pieces of garland together at the centres with blue string. The shorter piece will be the arms. The longer piece will be the legs.

3 Use a needle to poke a hole through the clown's head. Thread the blue string through the hole to attach the head to the body.

10

4 Cut a small piece of orange paper garland and glue it to the top of the clown's head for hair.

5 Cut a strip of red crepe paper and wrap it around the clown's body like a belt. Glue down the end of the crepe paper to hold it in place.

Wrap this string around your finger to make this clever clown dance.

Let your imagination soar

Other ideas:
You can also make the clown's head by wrinkling up tissue paper with a small amount of latex glue, or with newspaper mixed with water and latex glue (papier maché).

11

Curly Cat

This comical cat starts with a curl. Then all you have to do is add a cute face and a curvy tail.

Toolbox

You will need:
- black and white coloured pencils
- green cardboard
- glue stick
- scissors
- ruler

1 Measure a strip of green cardboard 5 cm wide and cut it out.

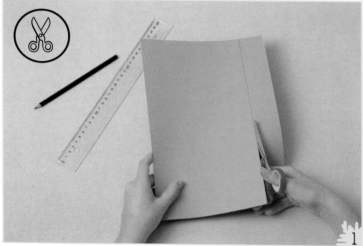

2 Fold the strip at 5 cm on one end and at 7.5 cm on the other end. Cut the short edge of the longer folded end into two rounded paws.

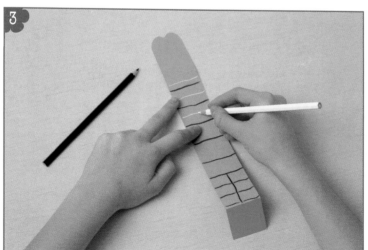

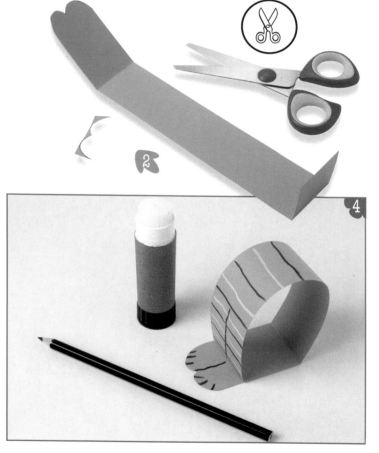

3 Draw black and white horizontal stripes from one fold to the other. Draw a vertical black line (as shown) to make legs.

4 Curl the strip around and glue the end down 5 cm behind the paws. Draw black claws and a line between the paws.

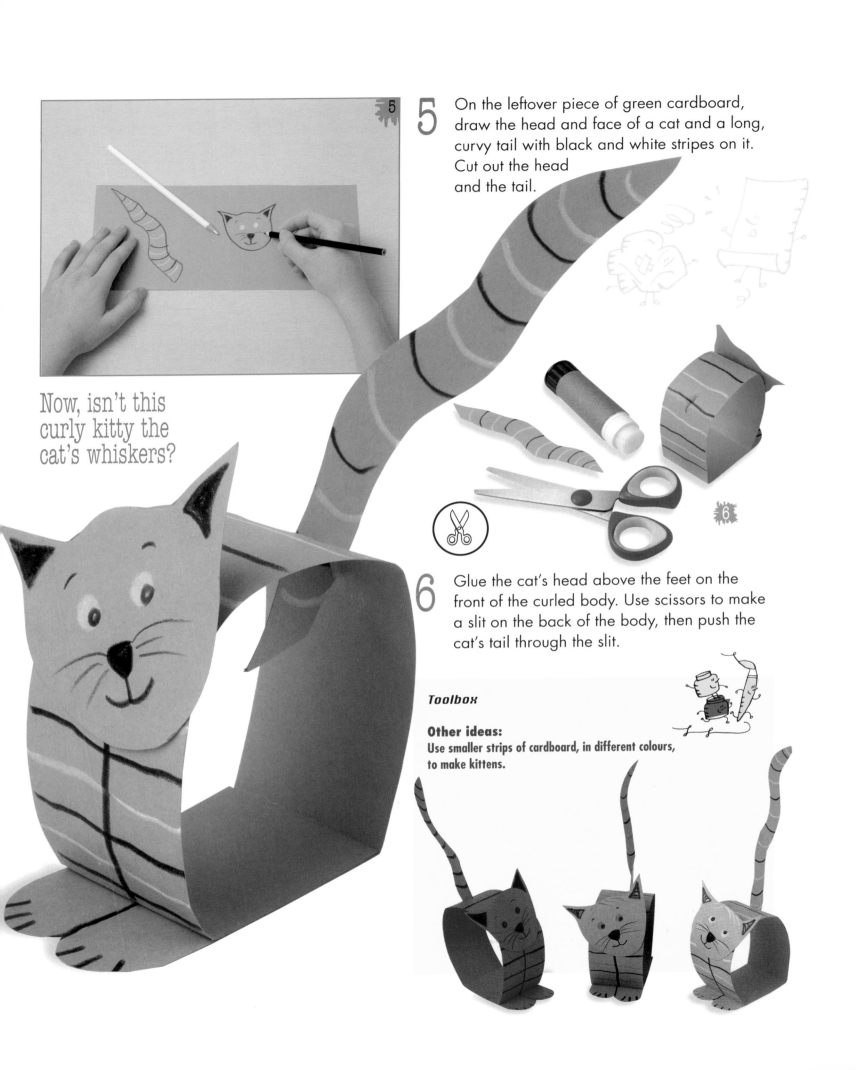

5 On the leftover piece of green cardboard, draw the head and face of a cat and a long, curvy tail with black and white stripes on it. Cut out the head and the tail.

Now, isn't this curly kitty the cat's whiskers?

6 Glue the cat's head above the feet on the front of the curled body. Use scissors to make a slit on the back of the body, then push the cat's tail through the slit.

Toolbox

Other ideas:
Use smaller strips of cardboard, in different colours, to make kittens.

Small-town
Scenery

Small-town
Scenery

Small-town Scenery

Set the stage for playtime with a town you build yourself out of cardboard and cut-outs. It's easy!

Toolbox

You will need:
- blue, green and red cardboard
- yellow, blue and brown wrapping paper
- square and rectangular coloured stickers
- sheet of white paper
- aluminium foil
- red tissue paper
- scissors
- coloured felt-tips
- glue stick
- ruler

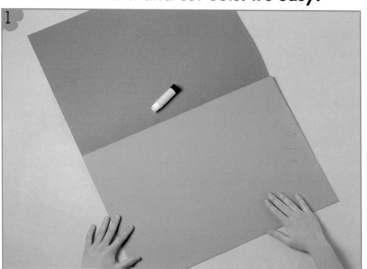

1 Cover the bottom half of a piece of blue cardboard with a piece of green cardboard and glue it in place.

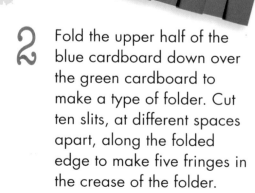

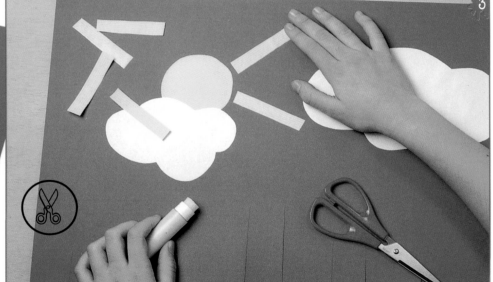

2 Fold the upper half of the blue cardboard down over the green cardboard to make a type of folder. Cut ten slits, at different spaces apart, along the folded edge to make five fringes in the crease of the folder.

3 Draw a sun on yellow wrapping paper and two clouds on a sheet of white paper, then cut them out. With the folder open, glue the sun and the clouds to the blue cardboard, which will be the sky.

14

4 Draw the shapes of two large houses and two small houses on red cardboard and cut them out.

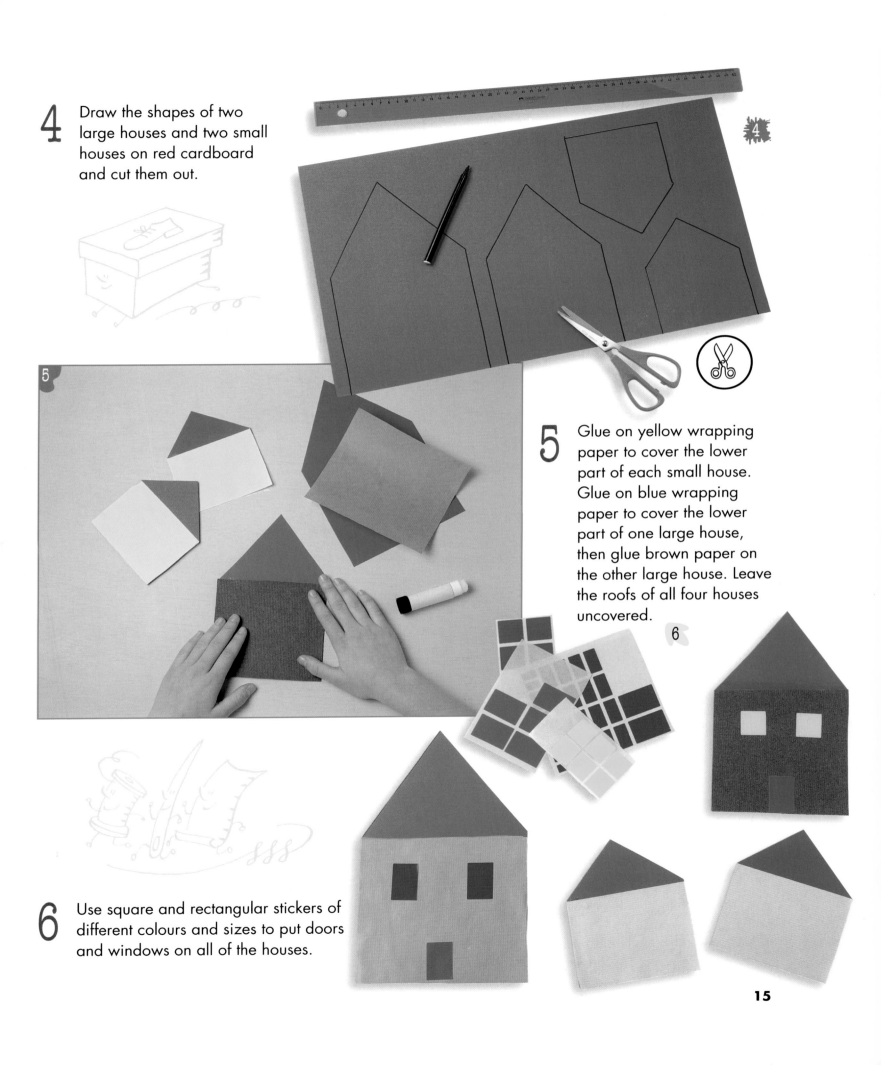

5 Glue on yellow wrapping paper to cover the lower part of each small house. Glue on blue wrapping paper to cover the lower part of one large house, then glue brown paper on the other large house. Leave the roofs of all four houses uncovered.

6 Use square and rectangular stickers of different colours and sizes to put doors and windows on all of the houses.

7 Draw the shape of a tree on green cardboard and cut it out. Glue on brown wrapping paper to cover the trunk.

8 Make little balls out of red tissue paper and glue them on the treetop to look like fruit.

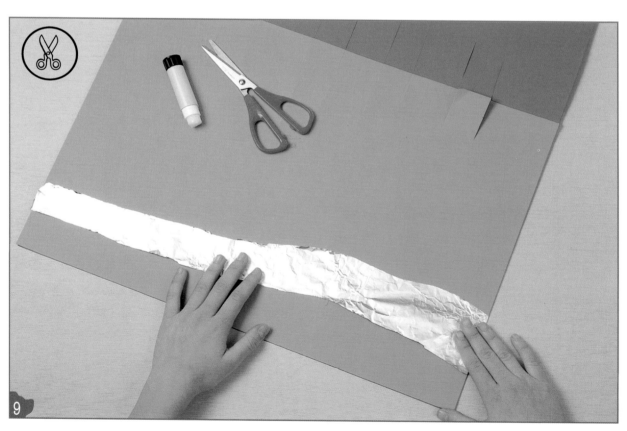

9 Cut a strip of aluminium foil and glue it across the green cardboard to make a river. The green cardboard will be grass-covered land.

16

10 Bend the sky forward at the crease, to stand upright with the fringes folding toward you. Glue the houses and the tree to the fringes, attaching one object to each fringe.

You have just constructed a small town! Make up some stories about it, then use your town as scenery to tell them.

Let your imagination soar

Other ideas:
Construct a city with skyscrapers, or a mountain scene, or a farm with animals.

Frilly Flower

Coloured crepe paper makes fabulous flowers! When you see how easy it is, you'll want to make a bunch.

2 Take a strip of each colour to make petals and attach it, with transparent tape, to one end of a wooden stick. Repeat the step two more times.

Toolbox

You will need:
- pink, red and purple crepe paper
- transparent tape
- thin, wooden stick
- green tissue paper
- scissors
- glue stick

1 Cut pink, purple and red crepe paper into short, wide strips. Cut three strips of each colour, then fold each strip in half.

3 Cut a long strip of green tissue paper.

18

4 Put glue on the strip and wrap it first around the bottom of the petals, then down the entire stick.

Combining many different colours of crepe paper will give you an endless variety of flowers.

5 Carefully open the folded crepe paper to make the petals of the flower blossom.

Let your imagination soar

Other ideas:
Make a bouquet of different coloured flowers with different stem lengths. Wrap the bouquet in a large piece of tissue paper.

Growing Girl

How would you like to make a paper doll that can actually grow? Impossible, you say? Not when you follow these instructions!

Toolbox

You will need:
- blue, red, yellow, orange, green, white and flesh-coloured paper
- long sheets of pink paper
- scissors
- glue stick
- black felt-tip

1 Fold two long sheets of pink paper into three sections. One sheet should be folded a little smaller than the other, so it will fit inside the larger folded sheet.

2 Draw a head with a long neck on a flesh-coloured piece of paper. Cut it out and glue it to the outside panel of the pink paper that is folded smaller.

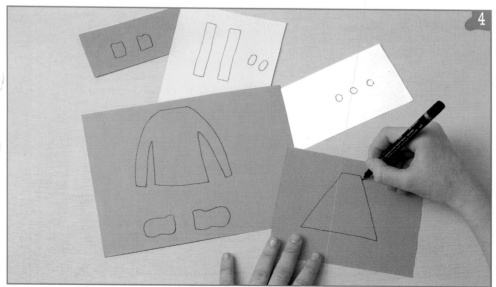

3 Use coloured paper to make blue eyes, a red nose and mouth, yellow hair and orange cheeks. Cut them out and glue them onto the head.

4 Using more coloured paper, make green shoes and a green shirt, white buttons, an orange skirt, blue socks and flesh-coloured legs and hands.

20

5 Cut out all the colour parts and glue them into the correct body positions onto the outside panel of the larger folded pink paper.

6 Insert the head panel into the body panel so it will slide in and out.

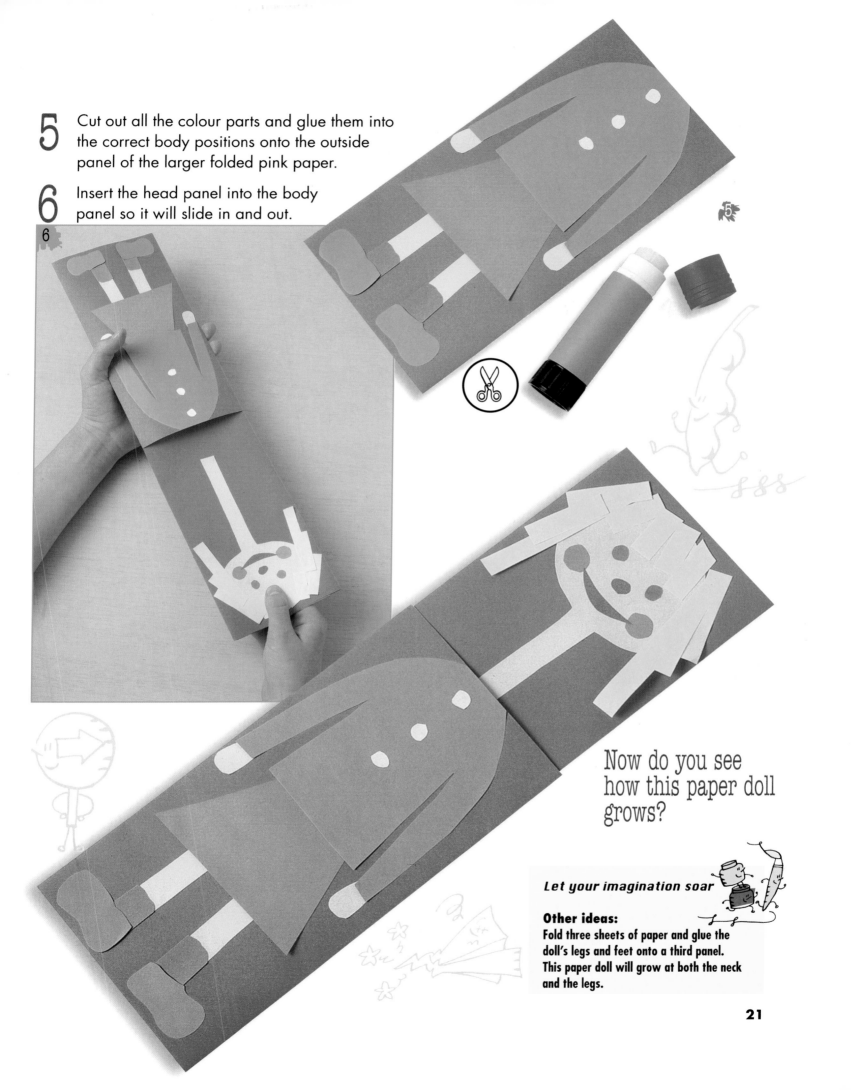

Now do you see how this paper doll grows?

Let your imagination soar

Other ideas:
Fold three sheets of paper and glue the doll's legs and feet onto a third panel. This paper doll will grow at both the neck and the legs.

Crafty Bag

Carrying books and toys around will be easier, and more fun, in this decorated bag.

Toolbox

You will need:
- blue, yellow and brown wrapping paper
- green circle stickers
- coloured felt-tip pens
- scissors
- glue stick

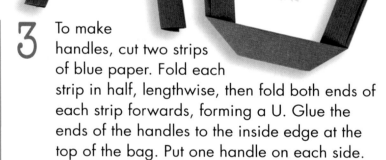

1 Cut a piece of blue paper 40 x 70 cm. Make a 10-cm flap on one long side. Fold one short side over 30 cm, then fold the other short side over it. Tuck one side of the top flap under the other, then glue the sides together.

2 To make the bottom of the bag, fold the corners at the end of the paper without the flap 5 cm inwards. Then fold that end up, making another flap, and glue it down.

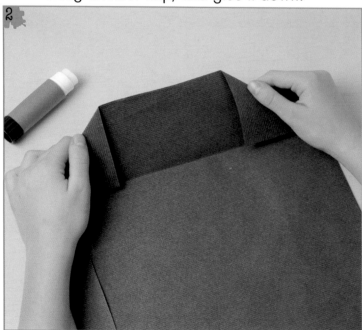

3 To make handles, cut two strips of blue paper. Fold each strip in half, lengthwise, then fold both ends of each strip forwards, forming a U. Glue the ends of the handles to the inside edge at the top of the bag. Put one handle on each side.

4 Draw the shape of a giraffe on a piece of yellow wrapping paper and cut it out.

22

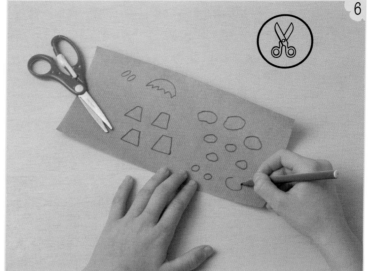

5 Glue the giraffe onto the bag. Put green circle stickers on its face for eyes and draw pupils on the stickers with a black felt-tip.

6 On brown wrapping paper, draw four hooves, a tail, two nostrils, a patch of hair and small spots of different sizes. Cut out each part and glue it in place on the giraffe's body.

You're done! You can use this colourful bag as a gift bag too.

Let your imagination soar

Other ideas:
Decorate bags with other animals you like or with pretty flowers.

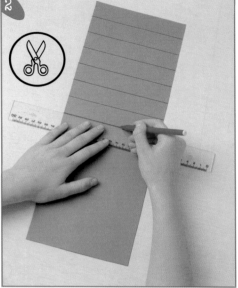

Day 'n' Night Dazzler

You can turn day into night with this magical work of art.

Toolbox

You will need:
- A4 (210 x 297 mm) sheet of white paper
- blue cardboard
- coloured pencils
- ruler
- glue stick
- coloured felt-tip
- scissors

1 Divide a sheet of white paper in half. On one half, draw a moon and stars (night). On the other half, draw a sun and clouds (day).

2 Cut a piece of blue cardboard 15 x 42 cm and draw lines across it, dividing it into fourteen 3-cm sections.

3 Fold the cardboard along each line, alternating the direction of the folds to make them look like a concertina.

4 Divide each drawing into seven 3-cm strips, then cut the strips apart.

5 Glue the strips onto the folds in the blue cardboard, alternating the strips, one at a time, from each drawing, in the correct order.

From now on, day and night will depend on which direction you're looking from.

Let your imagination soar

Other ideas:
Make two designs instead of two pictures.
Make one design with warm colours and
the other with cool colours.

Roly-poly Puppet

Turn a cardboard tube into a clever toy. All it takes is coloured paper, glue and imagination.

Toolbox

You will need:
- pink, blue, orange, purple and green sheets of paper
- cardboard tube from a roll of toilet paper
- small green and red circle stickers
- large white circle stickers
- glue stick
- scissors
- black felt-tip

1 Cut strips of pink, blue, purple and orange paper. Make each strip a different width.

2 Cut a narrow strip of green paper, then make triangular cuts along one side. Cut a wider strip of green paper and make small slits in one side, all the way across, to form a fringe.

3 Glue the strip of fringe around one end of a cardboard toilet paper tube. Then glue on the orange, purple, blue and pink strips, overlapping them. Glue the green strip with the triangular edge on last, around the bottom.

26

4 For eyes, draw a black dot (the pupil) inside each of two green circle stickers.

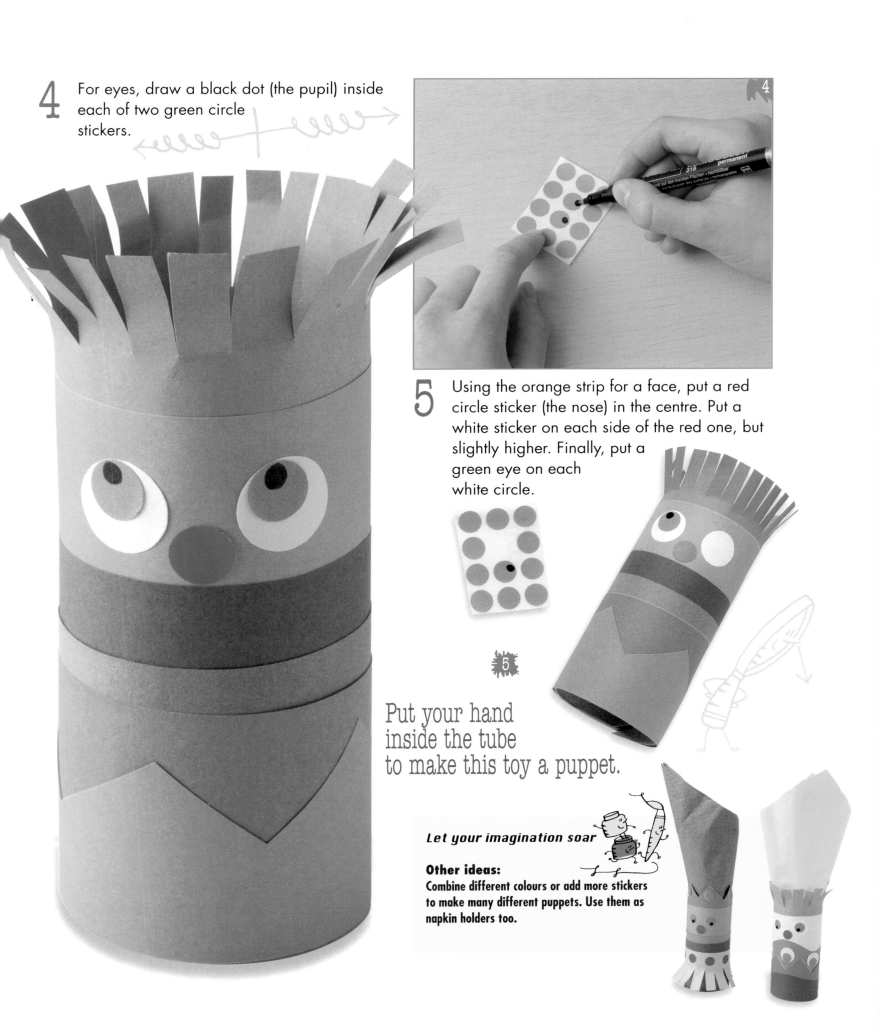

5 Using the orange strip for a face, put a red circle sticker (the nose) in the centre. Put a white sticker on each side of the red one, but slightly higher. Finally, put a green eye on each white circle.

Put your hand inside the tube to make this toy a puppet.

Let your imagination soar

Other ideas:
Combine different colours or add more stickers to make many different puppets. Use them as napkin holders too.

Telephone

With these instructions, you can make a telephone that looks almost real. It might even fool your friends.

Toolbox

You will need:
- red and black cardboard
- white rectangular stickers
- green circle stickers
- white pencil
- black felt-tip
- scissors
- ruler
- glue stick

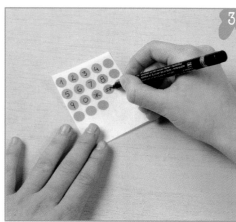

1 Cut a piece of red cardboard 11 x 18 cm. Draw lines 5, 8, 13 and 16 cm from one short edge. Fold the cardboard on each line. Glue the small flap left over at the end to the opposite edge to form a box.

2 Attach a white rectangular sticker at one end of one of the wide sides of the box. The sticker will be the screen.

3 Use a black felt-tip to draw numbers (0 to 9), an asterisk (*) and a hash mark (#) on green circle stickers. Draw one number or symbol on each sticker.

28

4 Stick the circles numbered 1 to 9 onto the phone, under the screen, in three rows. Make a fourth row with the *, the 0 and the # stickers.

5 With a white pencil, draw an antenna on black cardboard and cut it out. Glue the antenna to the top of the telephone.

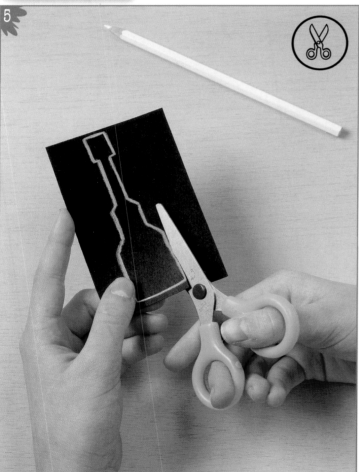

Let your imagination soar

Other ideas:
Make other accessories to add to your telephone or write numbers or a message on its screen.

Riiiing! Riiing! Time to take your first call on this tricky telephone.

Giant Sweet

Giant Sweet

Giant Sweet

Giant Sweet

Giant Sweet

Crinkly cellophane makes a fun-size sweet!

1 Roll up a yellow paper napkin, then wrap it in a piece of yellow cellophane. Twist the ends of the cellophane to make it look like a big boiled sweet.

2 Draw one circle on red cardboard (nose), two circles on blue cardboard (eyes) and two smaller circles on black cardboard (pupils for the eyes). Cut out all the circles.

Toolbox

You will need:
- yellow paper napkin
- yellow cellophane
- yellow, blue, black, yellow and green cardboard
- scissors
- transparent tape
- glue stick
- coloured felt-tip

3 Glue the eyes and the nose to the centre of the cellophane sweet to make a face.

4 Draw two legs and feet on yellow cardboard and cut them out.

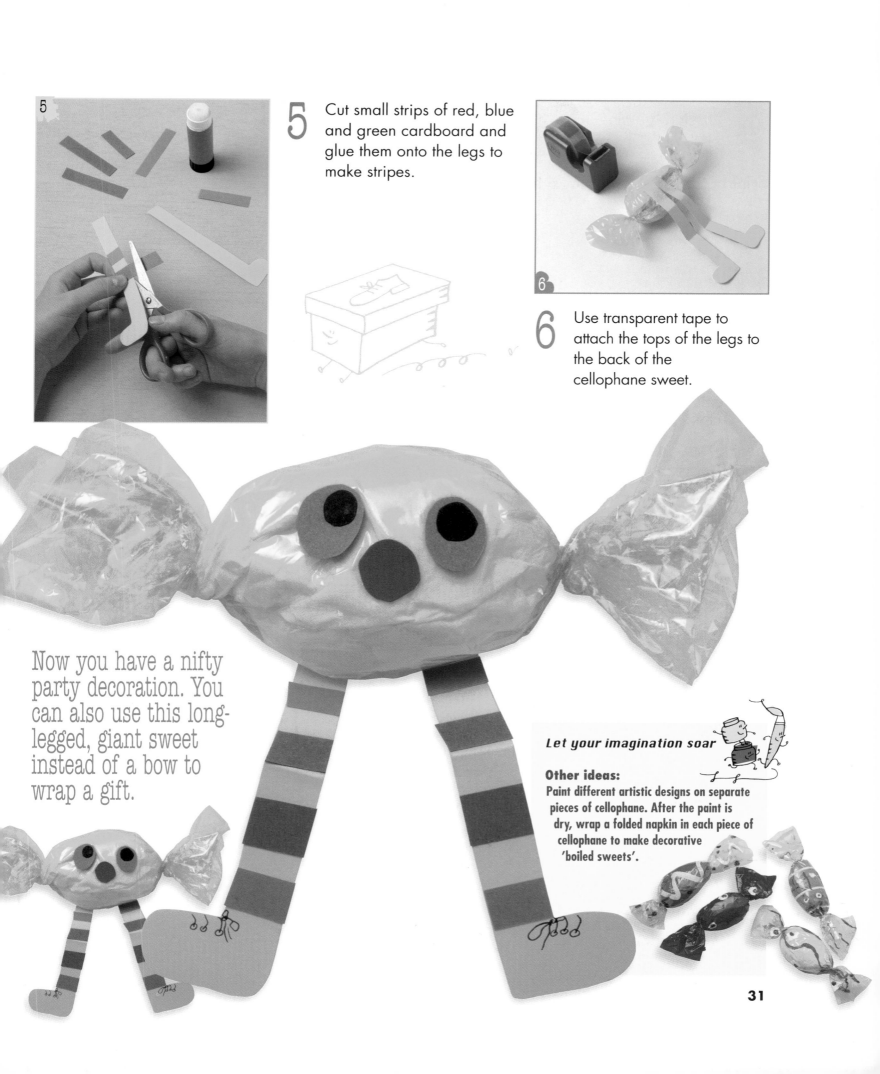

5 Cut small strips of red, blue and green cardboard and glue them onto the legs to make stripes.

6 Use transparent tape to attach the tops of the legs to the back of the cellophane sweet.

Now you have a nifty party decoration. You can also use this long-legged, giant sweet instead of a bow to wrap a gift.

Let your imagination soar

Other ideas:
Paint different artistic designs on separate pieces of cellophane. After the paint is dry, wrap a folded napkin in each piece of cellophane to make decorative 'boiled sweets'.

Make it with  Paper

Paper is an easy material to acquire and with which to do an infinite variety of handicrafts. An exercise with paper requires having to cut, draw, paint or paste, so a single task can bring together various learning experiences.

Following are some suggestions for making each project, as well as a guide to the most appropriate age level of each one. It is important to point out that the suggested age is based on the degree of difficulty of the process, but the projects can be easily adapted to varying age levels.

p.6 **Collage-covered Booklet.** Children can also do a collage, put a backing on it and use it as a coaster or as an individual placemat.
Ages 6 and up

p.8 **Carnival Hat.** When working with younger children, an adult should first make a cone. This will make the project shorter and easier to do.
Ages 5 and up

p.10 **Colourful Clown.** In place of the table-tennis ball for the head, a clay ball made by the child can be used.
Ages 6 and up

p.12 **Curly Cat.** Smaller children can be given the pieces of the cat already drawn so that they only have to cut, paint and paste them.
Ages 5 and up

p.14 **Small-town Scenery.** This project could be inspired by a specific subject that has been studied in class, e.g., traffic signals, types of trees or plants, food, etc.
Ages 6 and up

p.18 **Frilly Flower.** If thin, wooden sticks are not available, the stems of the flowers can be made by rolling up pieces of green paper or cardboard.
Ages 7 and up

p.20 **Growing Girl.** The same project can be done using coloured pencils or crayons to make it easier for smaller children.
Ages 5 and up

p.22 **Crafty Bag.** This project can also be done with younger children if readymade paper bags are used, since then they will only have to decorate them with wrapping paper.
Ages 6 and up

p.24 **Day 'n' Night Dazzler.** This craft activity encourages discussion about colours if cool tones are used for one drawing and warm tones for the other.
Ages 7 and up

p.26 **Roly-poly Puppet.** The project could be extended if children also decorate white paper with coloured borders and then use it to cover the tube.
Ages 5 and up

p.28 **Telephone.** For older children the project can be made a bit more complicated by telling them to cut out the screen on the telephone and pasting a piece of cellophane to it from behind, so that it is transparent.
Ages 6 and up

p.30 **Giant Sweet.** The 'sweets' can be filled with any sort of paper (newspaper, toilet paper, tissue paper) or with cotton wool. With a number of 'sweets' a mobile can be made to be hung from the ceiling.
Ages 5 and up